CONFLICT

CONFLICT
through the eyes of artists

Armed in a Civil War – © Miriam Macgregor

Wendy and Jack Richardson

© Heinemann Educational 1993
Apart from any fair dealing for the purposes of research or private study, or criticism or review, as permitted under the Copyright, Designs and Patents Act, 1988, this publication may only be reproduced, stored or transmitted, in any form or by any means, with the prior permission in writing of the publishers, or in the case of reprographic reproduction in accordance with the terms of licences issued by the Copyright Licensing Agency. Enquiries concerning reproduction outside those terms should be sent to the publishers at the undermentioned address.

Any person who does any unauthorized act in relation to this publication may be liable to criminal prosecution and civil claims for damages.

First published by Heinemann Library, 1993, a division of Heinemann Publishers (Oxford) Ltd, Halley Court, Jordan Hill, Oxford OX2 8EJ.

OXFORD LONDON EDINBURGH
MADRID PARIS ATHENS BOLOGNA
MELBOURNE SYDNEY AUCKLAND SINGAPORE TOKYO
IBADAN NAIROBI GABORONE HARARE
PORTSMOUTH NH (USA)

98 97 96 95 94
10 9 8 7 6 5 4 3 2

Series editing by Zoë Books Ltd
Picture research by Faith Perkins
Design by Mike Brain

Printed in China
British Library Cataloguing in Publication Data is available from the British Library on request.

ISBN 0-431-00978-3

Photographic acknowledgements
The authors and publishers wish to acknowledge with thanks the following photographic sources:
Cover and pp12–13: The Battle of San Romano – Reproduced by courtesy of the Trustees, The National Gallery, London
Title Page: Armed in a Civil War – © Miriam Macgregor
Frontispiece: Spencer – Self-Portrait – The Tate Gallery, London
Dragon confronting two Tigers – By courtesy of the Board of Trustees of the Victoria and Albert Museum, London. The Bridgeman Art Library pp6–7
Michelangelo by M. Venusti – Casa Buonarroti. Scala p8
David killing Goliath – The Sistine Chapel, Rome. Scala pp8–9
Brauner – Courtesy of the Mayor Gallery, London p10
The Consciousness of Shock (1951) – Peggy Guggenheim Collection, Venice (Solomon R. Guggenheim Foundation) Photograph David Heald. © DACS 1993 pp10–11
Uccello – Musée du Louvre, Paris © Photograph RMN p12

Picasso – National Gallery, Prague © DACS 1993 ARXIU MAS p14
Guernica – The Prado, Madrid © DACS 1993 ARXIU MAS pp14–15
Spencer – The Tate Gallery, London p16
The Resurrection of the Soldiers – National Trust. Photographic Library/A. C. Cooper p17
Amīr Hamza overthrows 'Amr i Ma'dī Kariba in Battle – Courtesy of The Ashmolean Museum, Oxford p19
Butler – The Mansell Collection p20
Balaclava – Manchester City Art Galleries pp20–1
Nolan – Camera Press, photograph Richard Open p22
The Death of Sergeant Kennedy at Stringybark Creek – Australian National Gallery, Canberra. Gift of Sunday Reed 1977. © Sir Sidney Nolan pp22–3
Raphael – Galleria degli Uffizi, Florence. Scala p24
The School of Athens – The Vatican, Rome. Scala pp24–5
Temptation of Christ on the Mountain – Copyright The Frick Collection, New York pp26–7
El Greco – Copyright © 1924 by The Metropolitan Museum of Art, New York p28
Christ Driving the Traders from the Temple – Reproduced by courtesy of The Trustees, the National Gallery, London pp28–9
Copley – The National Portrait Gallery, Smithsonian Institution, Washington DC p30
Charles I demanding the Surrender of the Five Impeached MPs – courtesy of The Trustees of the Public Library of The City of Boston pp30–1
Delacroix – Musée du Louvre, Paris. © Photograph RMN pp30–1
Liberty leading the People – Musée du Louvre, Paris. © Photograph RMN pp32–3
Daumier – © The Phillips Collection, Washington DC p34
The Uprising – © The Phillips Collection, Washington DC pp34–5
Kollwitz – National Gallery of Art, Washington DC © DACS 1993 p36
Rebellion of the Weavers. Print No 4 – Bildarchiv Preussischer Kulturbesitz © Prof. Dr. Arne A Kollwitz © DACS 1993 pp36–7
Nelson Mandela – © Photograph Gavin Younge. Thames and Hudson p39
Mr close-friend-of-the-family pays a visit whilst everyone else is out – © Sonia Boyce, Arts Council Collection pp40–1
Steen – Thyssen-Bornemisza Collection, Lugano, Switzerland p42
The Schoolmaster – The National Gallery of Ireland p43
Yeames – Mary Evans Picture Library p44
And When Did You Last See Your Father? – The Board of Trustees of the National Museums and Galleries on Merseyside (Walker Art Gallery) pp44–5

Portraits are by the artists themselves, unless stated otherwise.

The publishers have made every effort to trace the copyright holders, but if they have inadvertently overlooked any, they will be pleased to make the necessary arrangement at the first opportunity.

Contents

		PAGE
Introduction		5
Dragon confronting two Tigers	*Sadahide*	6
David killing Goliath	*Michelangelo*	8
The Consciousness of Shock (1951)	*Brauner*	10
The Battle of San Romano	*Uccello*	12
Guernica	*Picasso*	14
The Resurrection of the Soldiers	*Spencer*	16
Amīr Hamza overthrows 'Amr i Ma'dī Kariba in Battle	*unknown*	18
Balaclava	*Butler*	20
The Death of Sergeant Kennedy at Stringybark Creek	*Nolan*	22
The School of Athens	*Raphael*	24
Temptation of Christ on the Mountain	*Duccio*	26
Christ driving the Traders from the Temple	*El Greco*	28
Charles I demanding the Surrender of the Five Impeached MPs	*Copley*	30
Liberty leading the People	*Delacroix*	32
The Uprising	*Daumier*	34
Rebellion of the Weavers. Print No 4	*Kollwitz*	36
Nelson Mandela	*Malefane*	38
Mr close-friend-of-the-family pays a visit whilst everyone else is out	*Boyce*	40
The Schoolmaster	*Steen*	42
And When Did You Last See Your Father?	*Yeames*	44

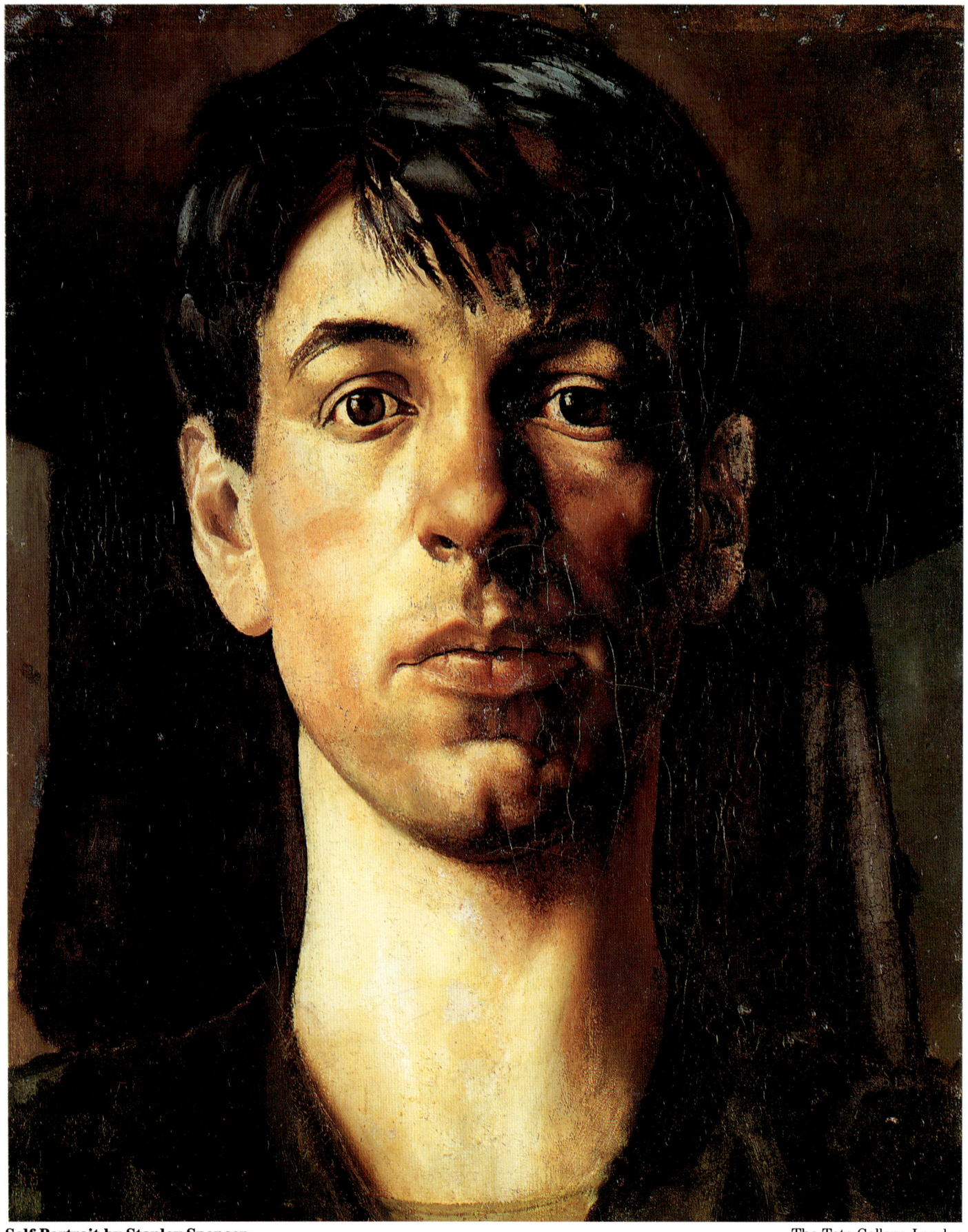

Self-Portrait by Stanley Spencer — The Tate Gallery, London

Introduction

This is a book of pictures about conflict. Some of the pictures are hundreds of years old and some of them were made quite recently. They come from all over the world. Some are paintings, some are drawings, some are prints. They look very different, but they have one thing in common. They were made by people who had an idea about conflict and thought that the best way to share that idea was through a picture. So this is a book for you to look at.

The pictures tell how the artists felt about different types of conflict. Some of the paintings are very serious. Others take a more light-hearted view. Some are about real events. Some are imaginary. Some are about physical conflict, others about the disagreement of ideas. Some are public conflicts, some are personal and private.

You will see how differently the idea of conflict has made each of the artists feel, and you will have different feelings yourself as you look at each of the pictures. Some of the pictures may make you feel that you agree with the artist – other pictures may show feelings that are very different from your own.

Some of the paintings are about events that you have probably never experienced such as a battle or a rebellion. Perhaps the paintings will help you to understand how it might have felt to be there. Some of the pictures show problems that you might meet in your life. Perhaps they will help you to understand your feelings about these problems.

For those who are interested in ideas

You may have chosen this book because you are interested in the idea of conflict. If so, perhaps you might think about conflicts in your life or environment and try making sense of them through drawing or painting. Like Picasso, you might show your anger at something. You might create symbols for good and bad in the modern world, like the painter of Nelson Mandela. You might think about problems at home or at school and use drawing to explain what you think is going on.

For picture lovers

You may have chosen this book because you like looking at pictures. If so, perhaps you would like to see the original works. A list at the beginning of the book tells you where to find those paintings which are on view to the public. They are in galleries all over the world, so you will not be able to see them all. However, your nearest gallery may have other works by the artists you like.

For those who want to have a go themselves

You may have chosen this book because you like to draw or paint. If so, perhaps it will help you to discover some of the secrets of picture making. All the work that is in the book is the result of hard thinking, lots of practice and above all very careful looking. Perhaps you could start a notebook now of the places and people around you. You could collect the information that will help you to make your own ideas come alive.

Dragon confronting two Tigers
print 36.5 x 71.8 cm
Sadahide

LIVED:
1807–1873

NATIONALITY:
Japanese

TYPE OF WORK:
prints

In this set of three prints the dragon and the tiger are symbols for elements of the weather. The breath of the tiger is the wind and the breath of the dragon is clouds. Their conflict makes the rain which brings life to earth. Dragon and tigers need to be equally matched. If the tigers' breath (the wind) is too strong, it will blow the dragon (the clouds) away and there will be no rain. If the dragon blows the tigers away there will be no wind and the earth will be flooded.

Print-making

In the eighteenth and nineteenth centuries printed pictures were very popular in Japan. Print-making was a team effort. The artist drew the outline of the picture onto thin paper which was then stuck onto a wooden block. The engravers cut the lines into the surface of the wood. The printer then made a few copies of the line drawing. The artist used these prints to decide what colours to use. A separate block was cut for each colour. Each block was then printed one on top of another.

The black ink for the line block was made from soot mixed with glue and the coloured inks from coloured powders mixed with rice paste. The paper was made from the fibres of the mulberry tree. It made a soft paper which absorbed the ink but was also strong and did not stretch. This made it easier for the printer to match each block exactly with the position of the one already printed. Matching the block is called registering.

The artists

The prints were always signed by the artist who was the designer of the work. This one was made by Sadahide who worked under the great master Kunisada. Some artists specialized in one type of print, but Sadahide did all sorts of work. His great skill is seen here in the wonderful textures of the animals, the leaf-like scales of the dragon and the softness of the tigers' stripes. The three sections form a continuous and harmonious picture. Against a dark background the sinuous cats and the mighty dragon are locked together like pieces in a jig-saw puzzle. Do you think it will rain?

By courtesy of the Board of Trustees of the Victoria and Albert Museum, London

David killing Goliath
Fresco height 243 cm
Michelangelo Buonarroti

LIVED:
1475–1564

NATIONALITY:
Italian

TYPE OF WORK:
painting, drawing, sculpture, architecture

Portrait M. Venusti. Casa Buonarroti

Michelangelo Buonarroti is one of the great figures of world art. He lived in Italy during the wonderful period of new learning and invention known as the Renaissance.

Michelangelo's most famous painting is on the ceiling of the Sistine Chapel in the Vatican Palace in Rome. He always said that he was a sculptor rather than a painter, and he tried to avoid painting. He did not want this work in the Sistine Chapel, but after he agreed to do it, the work seemed to take hold of him completely. It took four years to finish the project. From the moment the ceiling was revealed to the world it has caused amazement and wonder.

This section of Michelangelo's work shows David killing the giant Goliath. The painting is triangular and fits into the arch of a corner (a rounded corner like this is called a spandrel). Although it is only a tiny part of the whole ceiling, the painting is almost 2.5 metres high. The story shows that good can triumph over evil even if evil (Goliath) seems to be bigger and more powerful than good (David).

The young master

Michelangelo was 13 years old when he became an apprentice to the painter Ghirlandaio. Michelangelo learned drawing and fresco painting from Ghirlandaio, but soon the pupil outshone his master.

Michelangelo was fascinated by the sculptures from Ancient Greece and Rome which he studied in Florence. He wanted to know how to produce such lifelike energy and movement. The young artists of the Renaissance learned to combine imagination with scientific skills. They learned how the human body worked by dissecting corpses as well as by drawing from living models. Michelangelo soon understood perfectly how the human body worked. He knew exactly what it would look like in any position. His drawing talent was quickly recognized.

Michelangelo's great technical skill is shown in this painting, but his greatest gift was his imagination. He saw and painted in a way that helped people to understand more about themselves, about nature and about God.

The Sistine Chapel, Rome

The Consciousness of Shock (1951)
Encaustic on board 64 x 80 cm
Victor Brauner

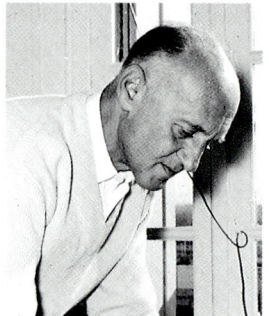

LIVED:
1903–1966

NATIONALITY:
Romanian

TYPE OF WORK:
painting

It takes some time to see what is going on in this picture. Two strange creatures – one bird-like, one human-like – seem to be sitting in a boat. Then we see that the two creatures and the boat may be all one creature. It seems to be fighting with itself. The long, thin neck of the human part of the creature is also the prow of the boat. The neck bends into the body, from which two feet stick out like paddles into the water. A second body, or section of body, with the wings, head and beak of a bird, forms the boat's stern. The bird end has stick-like arms with which it appears to be attacking its human end. The human end has three strong hands. With two hands it holds down the bird claws and with the third it paddles down the river.

Surreal images

Victor Brauner was born in Romania. He spent a short time at art school in Bucharest, then travelled to Paris, where he eventually settled in 1930. In Paris, Brauner met a group of painters known as the Surrealists. Their paintings showed that things are not always as they appear to be. They painted images from their dreams and imagination, as well as objects in the natural world around them. In this painting Brauner has created an unknown creature, but he has made it from bits of reality that we can recognize. Does it remind you of dreams or nightmares?

Links with ancient art

Brauner was interested in the paintings of artists who worked thousands of years ago. He used a flat painting style that he saw in ancient Egyptian and South American art. Here he seems to have had Egyptian wall paintings in mind.

During the Second World War Brauner lived in Switzerland. He had difficulty in finding paint, so he invented a waxy paint made from coloured candle grease. In fact this method of paint-making was used by the Ancient Greeks. Brauner spread the waxy colour over boards, then scratched lines into it. The method is called graffito, and the word 'graffiti' comes from it.

Peggy Guggenheim Collection, Venice. Photograph © 1991
The Solomon R. Guggenheim Foundation © DACS 1993

Niccolo Maurizzo da Tolentino at the Battle of San Romano
Tempera on wooden panel 182 x 320 cm
Paolo di Dono (called Uccello)

Musée du Louvre, Paris

LIVED:
c. 1396–1475

NATIONALITY:
Italian

TYPE OF WORK:
mosaics and paintings

Paolo di Dono lived at a time when artists and scholars were rediscovering the work of the Greeks and Romans. This renewal of interest became known as the rebirth or Renaissance. Many artists were interested in the problem of painting objects so that they looked real and solid on the flat surface of a canvas. How could they paint scenes that showed distance? Paolo di Dono spent years trying to work out rules that would help other artists to understand how to make accurate drawings. These rules are called rules of perspective.

Perspective drawing was one love of Paolo's life. The other was his love of animals and birds. His nickname 'Uccello' means 'bird'.

A training for a painter
When he was about ten years old, Uccello was apprenticed to the famous sculptor Ghiberti. It may have been this early training which made him interested in how to paint figures that look rounded, almost as though they are carved rather than painted.

The great battle scene
This picture is one of three paintings Uccello made for a palace in Florence. The battle of San Romano had taken place 25 years before Uccello painted the pictures. In a way, he uses the subject simply to make a decorative painting, showing lots of energy and excitement. On the white horse, the hero of Florence, Niccolo da Tolentino, leads his army to victory against the knights of Siena.

The picture's perspective
Uccello has succeeded in giving his picture depth. The smaller figures in the background do look further away than the larger figures. The broken lances on the ground lead our eyes into the picture, which helps to give it depth. Uccello also wanted to make his figures look three-dimensional. He used the technique called 'foreshortening' to do this. The figure of the knight on the ground is a good example of a foreshortened figure.

Reproduced by courtesy of the Trustees, The National Gallery, London

Guernica
Oil on canvas 348 x 777 cm
Pablo Ruiz y Picasso

National Gallery, Prague © DACS 1993

LIVED:
1881–1973

NATIONALITY:
Spanish, lived much of his life in France

TYPE OF WORK:
paintings, drawings, sculptures, ceramics, prints

Pablo Ruiz y Picasso was a brilliant draughtsman and painter. By the time he was 16 years old he had learned all that he could at the art schools in Spain. When he was 19 he made his first visit to Paris. He settled there two years later, but always thought of himself as a Spaniard.

The tireless worker

Picasso was adventurous in his work. He gobbled up ideas from everywhere, seeing the world with a clear, fresh eye. When he died in 1973, aged 92, he had made thousands of drawings and paintings. He had filled 175 notebooks with sketches, observations and ideas, and it was upon this collection of information that he built his most important works.

Anger creates a painting

In 1936 civil war broke out in Spain. In April 1937 Picasso heard of the terrible daytime bombing of Guernica, a small town in northern Spain. Picasso was outraged. His anger inspired him to paint one of the fiercest pictures of war that has ever been made. Instantly he began to draw to bring his vision to life. He pulled images from his memory and combined them in sketch after sketch until he found a way to express his feelings. Just ten days after he made the first sketch, Picasso put up an enormous canvas in his studio. He worked quickly, outlining his ideas. The first plan changed often during the two months he took to paint the picture. Figures came and went or were moved about until he was satisfied. Soon, the woman with the lamp, the horse and the bull appeared. From the very beginning Picasso was sure that he wanted the terrified horse. He painted it in many different ways until he was satisfied with it charging through the centre of the picture. He painted large bold areas of white against dull greens and greys. The effect is hard, sharp and cruel.

The Prado, Madrid © DACS 1993

The Resurrection of the Soldiers
Oil on canvas 628 x 498 cm
Stanley Spencer

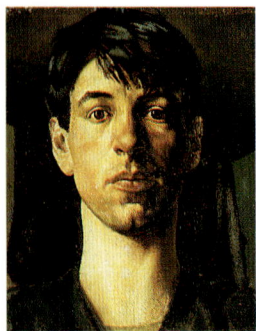

The Tate Gallery, London

LIVED:
1891–1959

NATIONALITY:
British

TYPE OF WORK:
paintings

Stanley Spencer was a religious and an imaginative man. In his work he combined images of the world he saw around him with the expression of religious ideas.

During the First World War Spencer served as a medical orderly in Greece. The scenes he saw there remained clear in his memory and later became a plan for a set of pictures. He met a wealthy couple who greatly admired his plan. They decided to build a chapel in memory of a brother who was killed in the war, and they asked Spencer to paint his pictures for the chapel.

Life after the conflict

The side walls of the chapel show scenes from the everyday life on the battlefield. Some show wounded men and life in hospital. Others show men in the trenches, or in field camps, cooking, amusing themselves, or collecting water.

The largest picture is behind the altar on the east wall. The dead cover the picture from top to bottom in a torn and broken landscape. Yet this is not a scene of death. Spencer is showing the Christian belief that there is life after death. Soldiers and mules return to life in quietness and calm, amidst the confusion of crosses and the jumble of bodies. Faces are puzzled, not angry. Hands reach out in greeting. One soldier touches a strolling tortoise, one reads — maybe a letter from home. There is no haste, for this is Eternity.

Planning the picture

Spencer developed the idea for the crosses when he was drawing a grid of lines over a canvas. He saw places where the grid lines crossed and thought that they were like frames around portraits as well as being the symbol with which Christians mark graves.

Like Picasso, Spencer has built his picture on a triangle. Guernica has a lamp, a symbol of hope, at its apex. For Spencer the apex is the figure of Christ who receives the crosses from the risen dead.

© The National Trust 1993

Amīr Hamza overthrows 'Amr i Ma'dī Kariba in Battle

Gouache on cloth 67 x 49.5 cm
Artist unknown

DATE:
c 1562

PLACE:
Mughal India

This picture comes from India and is an illustration for a story called the Hamza-nama. Amīr Hamza was an uncle of the Muslim prophet Muhammed and the book tells of his adventures. The whole book had 1400 pictures painted on pages made from cotton. There were once 14 volumes of the book, but today only 200 pages are left. The book took about 15 years to complete and this was one of the earliest paintings to be finished.

A heroic tale

This scene was painted about 100 years after Uccello painted his battle scenes. It is just as busy and energetic. The rider in this picture is the giant warrior 'Amr i Ma'dī Kariba. Hamza, the young hero of the tale, is on the black horse. He is so brave and strong that he has pushed the warrior over with his foot. Soldiers from both sides look on in astonishment at such a feat of strength.

The book was made for Akbar, ruler of the Mughal Empire in the north of India from 1556 to 1605. Akbar was a strong and wise emperor. He was interested in the people he ruled and their customs and religion. He was also interested in art and poetry and he enjoyed the traditional stories of his people.

Combining three styles

Akbar set up a studio in his court, bringing Persian painters to work there and employing a Persian master to direct it. He also encouraged Indian painters to come to the studio to work with the Persians. Soon a new style had developed. This was a mixture of Persian and Indian ideas and of the ideas from Europe that were just reaching India. The style had the elegance and beauty of the Persian work, the liveliness of Indian work and the naturalistic quality of European work.

This painting shows the beginning of the mixture of influences. The rocky background, the big skyline and the decorative tree show the Persian tradition. The lively figures, especially the musicians at the top of the picture, are much more Indian.

Do you think that this picture was meant to make people think seriously about war? How do you feel when you look at it?

Courtesy of The Ashmolean Museum, Oxford

Balaclava

Oil on canvas 103.4 x 187.5 cm
Elizabeth Thompson, Lady Butler

LIVED:
1846–1933

NATIONALITY:
British

TYPE OF WORK:
large paintings

This painting shows the suffering of war. Butler painted many pictures of famous battles, and shocked the public who did not believe a woman could (or should) paint such scenes.

'I never painted for the glory of war . . .'

Butler's paintings do not show war as something grand. She often concentrated on the time just after battle. She said, 'I never painted for the glory of war, but to portray its pathos and heroism.' She is also said to be the first British artist to paint ordinary soldiers, instead of officers and generals.

Bringing back memories of battle

Butler had no personal experience of battles, but she took extreme care to get the details right. She was wealthy and was able to hire horsemen as models and to have costumes made. Once she even bought a field of rye and had it trampled, so that she could see exactly what it might look like after a battle. *Balaclava* was painted in 1875, about 20 years after the actual event, but the artist had talked to old soldiers about their memories of the battle. Some veterans were upset when they saw the work. The artist had understood them so well that the painting brought back all the dreadfulness and suffering of the battle itself.

Admiration and surprise

Butler may have shocked the public but she also won their admiration. She certainly surprised John Ruskin, one of the art critics of the time. He had said that no woman could paint! Butler changed his mind.

The shape of Butler's painting is similar to Uccello's battle scene. Both have a strong pyramid of horsemen on the right of the picture and a lesser one to the left. In both, lances and flags take the eye up and down the picture, but the flags fly quite differently. Butler's flags droop despondently, while Uccello's swirl above his hero's head.

Again we see fallen horses and falling men. Which of the five battle pictures makes you feel most strongly? What messages do you think each artist was trying to give us?

© Manchester City Art Galleries

The Death of Sergeant Kennedy at Stringybark Creek
Enamel on composition board 91 x 121.7 cm
Sidney Nolan

BORN:
1917

NATIONALITY:
Australian

TYPE OF WORK:
painting, theatre design, illustration, film

In 1870 a band of outlaws roamed the Australian state of Victoria. They were Ned Kelly, his brother Dan, Joe Byrne and Steve Hart. The gang wore home-made armour to protect themselves from bullets. As they were hunted through the bush, several policemen were killed. Finally the gang was tricked and captured and Ned Kelly, aged only 25, was hanged at Melbourne gaol. He is remembered in Australia in much the same way that the cowboy outlaws of the American 'wild west' are remembered, with a mixture of horror for their deeds and admiration for their daring. They are heroes and villains at the same time.

A legend comes to life
Sidney Nolan, a painter from Melbourne, grew up hearing the story of Ned Kelly's gang. He was fascinated by Kelly's character — the conflict between the good and the bad, the cowardly and the fearless sides of the outlaw. In 1945 Nolan went to visit 'Kelly country'. He started painting the story of the gang and their capture and in two years he had painted 27 pictures. This set of paintings, perhaps Nolan's most famous work, spread the story of Ned Kelly across the world.

The legend and the landscape
Nolan has a deep understanding and love for the shapes and colours of the Australian landscape. Most of the Ned Kelly paintings are set in the bush. The figures stand out starkly in the open landscape. The dry, unwelcoming land seems to emphasize the harshness of the story.

Nolan chose to paint the figures simply, like comic characters or puppets. Kelly especially, in his metal mask, seems to have become less than human. In some of the paintings, the sky is seen through the eye-piece of the helmet, suggesting that the head is empty. The policemen are also wooden, like toy soldiers. They obey the orders. They have no choice.

Nolan has returned to this story many times. He has also continued to paint the bush, the varied landscape of other Australian states, and different stories from Australia's past.

Reproduced by permission of the Australian National Gallery, Canberra. Gift of Sunday Reed 1997 © Sir Sidney Nolan

The School of Athens
Fresco width at base 770 cm
Raffaello Sanzio (known as Raphael)

LIVED:
1483–1520

NATIONALITY:
Italian

TYPE OF WORK:
painting and architecture

Galleria degli Uffizi, Florence

Raphael was a professional painter by the time he was 16 years old. When he was only 25 he travelled to Rome. The Pope had asked him to paint the walls of one of the rooms in the Vatican Palace.

The link with the past
The theme of the room is the link between the learning of the Greeks and Romans and the later teachings of Christianity. The paintings are very large, each covering an entire wall. Many of the figures in the paintings are life-size. The pictures balance each other in shape, in movement and colour.

In this huge, almost semi-circular picture, we see the learned scholars of classical Greece. In the centre stand the philosophers (thinkers), Plato and Aristotle. Everyone is deep in thought or discussion. The picture illustrates another type of conflict, the conflict of ideas.

Painting a world that looks real
Raphael achieved everything that the artists of the Renaissance struggled for. He could make a flat surface look as if we could walk into it. In this painting it seems possible that we could walk past the people on the steps, right up to Plato and Aristotle and on beyond them.

Raphael could paint people so that they appear to be made of solid flesh beneath their clothing. Their gestures seem natural and light. It is almost as if we can see the rest of their movements. He could paint people sitting, standing, kneeling, lazing. He could paint them on the move. Look at Plato and Aristotle. Do they seem to be coming towards you? Raphael balanced his pictures perfectly so that nothing seems out of place, nowhere is crowded, nowhere seems empty. He focuses our eyes where he wants them to look.

Raphael was a master of colour, of perspective and of composition. Compare this painting with Duccio's *Temptation of Christ on the Mountain* to see what enormous changes had come about in painting technique in 200 years.

The Vatican, Rome

Temptation of Christ on the Mountain
Tempera on wooden panel 43 x 46 cm
Duccio de Buoninsegna

LIVED:
1278–1319

NATIONALITY:
Italian

TYPE OF WORK:
religious painting

Duccio de Buoninsegna worked before the time of the Italian Renaissance. Like all great artists he was searching for better ways of expressing ideas. Duccio was part of a tradition of religious painting in which pictures of God, Jesus and the saints were thought to be almost holy in themselves. People thought that God showed himself to the people through the work of the artist. This responsibility had frightened some picture-makers. Artists and churchmen did not want to take any risks if they were showing God Himself. The pictures were beautiful but the same poses, the same expressions, the same ornaments were used time and again. Strict rules governed the way everything looked. Duccio tried to break away from these restrictions.

New ways of thinking and seeing
In Italy in the thirteenth century painters were beginning to have new ideas. The human characteristics of Christ and his disciples were being discussed. Duccio wanted to express these ideas in his work. He looked for inspiration at real people, at their movements and especially their faces, which showed their feelings. He thought of his paintings not so much as pictures of Christ himself, but as pictures of events in Christ's life. Duccio created new and exciting pictures, but he did not abandon the old style completely. He brought a new spirit into the traditional forms of painting.

This painting comes from a set which Duccio painted for the cathedral in Siena. It is part of an enormous altarpiece. On the front was a picture of the Virgin Mary with the baby Jesus. On the back are scenes from the life of Christ. This scene shows Jesus in conflict with the devil himself, on a mountain top in the wilderness. The conflict is a battle of wills. The devil is offering Jesus all that he can see but Jesus sends him away. He does not want earthly power.

Jesus, the angels and even the devil are painted to look like real personalities. They contrast strongly with the strange lumpy landscape and the toytown buildings. In Duccio's time artists had not yet begun to try out new ways of painting background.

Duccio did not work alone. Some experts think that the painter Pietro Lorenzetti may have worked on this scene.

Copyright The Frick Collection, New York

Christ driving the Traders from the Temple

Oil on canvas 106 x 129 cm

Domenicos Thetocopoulos (known as 'El Greco', the Greek)

LIVED:
c. 1544–1614

NATIONALITY:
Greek, but worked in Italy and Spain

TYPE OF WORK:
painter, architect, sculptor

The Metropolitan Museum of Art, New York

El Greco was born on the Greek island of Crete. He studied in Venice with the painters Tintoretto and Titian, then he moved to Spain where he spent the rest of his working life. El Greco's style is unmistakable. His figures are tall and slender, clothed in billowing drapery, and lit by a cold white light. His style was not popular amongst the aristocrats at the Spanish court. It was the church that kept El Greco in work. His pictures had a mysterious spiritual quality, a little frightening and very powerful, which suited the religious feelings in Spain at that time.

Powerful feelings

In this picture the conflict between Jesus and the traders is violently expressed. We see Jesus turning on the traders in the temple and driving them out. His eyes are wide with rage. He lashes out with the rope whip in his hand. An overturned table lies at his feet. The traders cringe and hide from the blows.

A careful composition

El Greco has put this picture together very carefully. Jesus stands upright in the centre of the picture, a head taller than anyone else. The pillars of the temple echo the line of his figure. The rich red of his costume, the only red in the picture, focuses attention on him and conflicts with the strength of the yellows around him.

The other figures are pale beside Jesus. They lean away or kneel towards him. They have been carefully placed on diagonal lines which reach from the corners of the picture to Christ at the centre, making a very strongly shaped picture.

El Greco had painted this subject at least twice while he was working in Italy. He learned a great deal from paintings he saw there. For instance, there are likenesses between the poses of his figures and those of Michelangelo's figures. But the ideas of Tintoretto appealed most to El Greco. Tintoretto cared more for the story-telling power of a picture than for its 'beauty' and his work shocked many people.

Reproduced by courtesy of the Trustees, The National Gallery, London

Charles I demanding the Surrender of the Five Impeached MPs

Oil on canvas 233.7 x 312.4 cm
John Singleton Copley

LIVED:
1737–1815

NATIONALITY:
American (USA)

TYPE OF WORK:
paintings

The National Portrait Gallery, Smithsonian Institution, Washington DC

This painting shows a very important moment in British history. It is about a conflict between King Charles I and his Parliament. It was not their first quarrel, and it was to lead to civil war and to Charles's defeat and death. The painting is about power. It captures the moment when King Charles entered Parliament and demanded the arrest of five of its members. The Speaker refused to hand them over. The gestures of the Speaker and the King (with the hat) show us that they are arguing. Around them a sea of shocked faces waits to see what will happen.

An American breaks with tradition

John Singleton Copley was born in Boston in North America. His stepfather was an engraver, but Copley taught himself to paint. In 1774 he left America for Europe and settled in London. There he quickly adopted the style of the fashionable painter. Paintings at that time were usually about religious subjects, or stories from ancient history. Sometimes the artists represented ideas about goodness, truth and beauty through story-like scenes. Copley had not been brought up in this tradition and he felt free to choose any subject to paint. When a friend suggested this historical subject, Copley's interest was caught.

Accurate research

Copley took great pains to make sure that the details of his painting were accurate. He consulted historians for information on costume and the parliament building of the time. He even visited country houses to see portraits of Members of Parliament who were known to have been present on the day. The painting caused a great stir when it was first shown. Not only was it most unusual to paint a fairly recent historical event, it was unheard of to make it look real and to paint it as if the viewer might have been there.

In the next century historical subjects became very popular and many artists tried to bring the past to life as Copley had done.

Courtesy of the Trustees of the Boston Public Library

Liberty leading the People
Oil on canvas 260 x 325 cm
Eugene Delacroix

LIVED:
1798–1863

NATIONALITY:
French

TYPE OF WORK:
paintings, drawings, murals

Musée du Louvre, Paris

Eugene Delacroix lived in France at a time of terrible turmoil. Most of his paintings are of stories from long ago or are romantic views of life in far-away countries. This painting is one of the few he painted of the events happening around him. In 1830 there was an uprising which brought to power the Emperor Louis Philippe. Delacroix painted the uprising as it was happening. He did not avoid the horrors of the fighting, but used his highly dramatic style to express a point of view. It is a political painting.

In the centre of the painting, shown in the strongest colours, is the flag of France, the Tricolore. It is held high by Liberty, the symbol of France and of the freedom of the people. Bare-chested and bare-footed, strong and fearless, Liberty waves the flag with one hand and a gun with the other. She rallies the people around her and leads them on, striding to victory over the bodies of the uniformed enemy. Following her are the two sections of French society — the workers and the *bourgeoisie* or middle classes — who joined ranks to bring Louis Philippe to power. The man in the top hat and black coat represents the *bourgeoisie*, fighting alongside the working people. Sadly this alliance lasted for only a short time.

A classical training

Delacroix's mother came from a family of craftworkers and designers. When he was eighteen he became a pupil in an artist's studio, where he learned his skills through copying great paintings. His favourite painter was Rubens.

Delacroix worked very hard. He always made many large drawings in preparation for each painting, and numerous smaller ones. When he died, thousands of paintings and drawings were found in his studio. He was proud of his speed in drawing. He said, 'If you are not skilful enough to sketch a man falling out of the window during the time it takes him to get from the fifth storey to the ground, then you will never be able to produce monumental work.'

Musée du Louvre, Paris

The Uprising

Oil on canvas 87.6 x 113 cm
Honoré Daumier

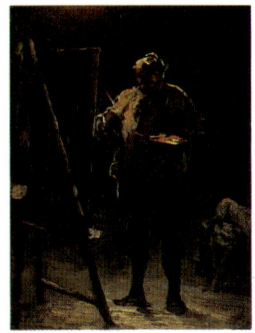

LIVED:
c. 1808–1879

NATIONALITY:
French

TYPE OF WORK:
lithographs, engravings, watercolours, oil paintings

The Phillips Collection, Washington DC

When Honoré Daumier died in 1879 he left more pictures than any other known artist. Until he was 52 years old, Daumier earned his living by drawing for the newspapers. This type of work was popular at a time before photographs could be easily reproduced.

Comments on the times

Daumier's newspaper drawings commented sharply on the politics and politicians of the day. He spent six months in prison in 1832 because his drawings of the French Emperor, Louis Philippe, were so critical. Then he drew popular actors, art critics and ordinary working people, but when there was an uprising in 1848, Daumier returned to politics. This painting was made several years after the conflict but is probably based on the artist's experiences of that time.

The cartoonist turns to painting

Although Daumier earned his living from his drawings, he really wanted to paint. However, his paintings were not generally popular. It seemed that only other artists thought the work was good. In the last years of his life Daumier's sight failed, but the kindness of another painter saved him from total poverty.

Daumier's training in art had been gathered in various places. He was apprenticed to a printer to learn a new method called lithography. Drawings were made on flat slabs of stone with wax crayon. The stone was wetted, but the water ran off the waxed parts. Then the stone was covered in greasy ink, but this time the wet parts repelled the ink. Now paper could be pressed on to the stone and the drawing was transferred to the paper. Daumier was one of the first artists to use the new method well.

Daumier had studied sculpture but he had no training in oil painting. He worked on canvas in the way that he had on stone, smudging paint into areas of light and darkness and making the shapes strong by drawing. We can see the influence of his lithography and his sculpture in his paintings. His figures have the sort of strength that monuments have, but they are also very much alive.

© The Phillips Collection, Washington DC

Rebellion of the Weavers. Print No 4
Etching 21.9 x 23.5 cm
Käthe Kollwitz

Self-portrait at the Table; Käthe Kollwitz; National Gallery of Art, Washington; Rosenwald Collection © DACS 1993

LIVED:
1867–1945

NATIONALITY:
German

TYPE OF WORK:
drawing, print-making and sculpture

Käthe Kollwitz was 13 years old when she first learned to make prints. From then on she preferred drawing and printing to painting.

Kollwitz was very concerned about injustice. She wanted help to be given to the needy and she thought that poor people deserved a greater share of the country's wealth. Kollwitz married a doctor who worked in a very poor part of Berlin. There she saw people living in dreadful conditions and decided to do what she could to help.

Pictures of political beliefs

Kollwitz's beliefs formed the subjects for her work. In 1893 she saw a play called 'The Weavers', about a true event from the recent past. Hand-loom weavers were threatened by new machinery and feared that they would lose their jobs. They rebelled. Kollwitz worked on the idea for four years and in 1898 she produced a series of six prints. They caused a sensation because they were so good, and a scandal because of their political subject matter. This is the fourth of the series. It shows the weavers — men and women with pinched and desperate faces — marching determinedly, armed with picks and axes. One shakes a defiant fist and shouts to encourage the others.

The exhibition jury of the Prussian Academy of Arts wanted to give her the gold medal for her work. However, the German Emperor, the Kaiser, was not at all pleased and would not allow the medal to be awarded to her.

The power of black and white

Kollwitz worked in black and white because she believed in the power and strength of line-drawing. She also wanted the people who were her subjects to be able to buy her work. If many copies of a work are printed they are much cheaper than a painting.

This work is an etching. Etchings like this have the same sort of look as pencil drawings.

Bildarchiv Preussischer Kulturbesitz © Prof. Dr. Arne A Kollwitz © DACS 1993

Nelson Mandela
Oil on canvas size not known
Matthew 'M K' Malefane

BORN:
1958

NATIONALITY:
South African

TYPE OF WORK:
painting and film-making

Painting a picture gives people a chance to say what they feel about something. Sometimes the feeling comes direct from the artist's own, personal experiences. Sometimes an artist wants to identify with the experience of a people or a well-known figure. Many South African artists have used their art to express their feelings about the injustices of *apartheid* and what it has done to all the people.

A powerful symbol
Nelson Mandela is probably the best known South African name in the world. Mandela spent most of his life in gaol because of his opposition to *apartheid*. He has come to be a symbol for people struggling to be free, wherever they are. When Mandela was finally released from prison, his own people rejoiced and the world marvelled at a man who could be so determined for so many years.

A choice?
The painting shows Mandela through broken and twisted prison bars. He is standing in a box, which looks like a pulpit in a church. Like a preacher, Mandela raises his eyes to heaven and lifts one hand in a dramatic gesture. But words, used by preachers and politicians, are not the only way to win an argument. In his other hand he holds a spear, the soldier's weapon of both defence and attack.

Behind Mandela hangs the flag of the African National Congress. The yellow stripe behind Mandela's head darkens towards the edge. The effect is to give Mandela a halo, or perhaps to stand him in the rising sun, a symbol for a new hope and new beginnings. Mandela's shirt has become a seascape. In the distance we see an island. A swimmer nearing the shore is surrounded by sharks. Mandela served his prison sentence on Robben Island. Is Mandela the swimmer? Who do you think the sharks might be?

'M K' Malefane was born in Soweto. He attended Lesotho High School and later studied film-making in Cape Town. He now works as a documentary film-maker in Johannesburg. Malefane taught himself to paint. This picture made a deep impression on black African viewers who immediately understood its clear message.

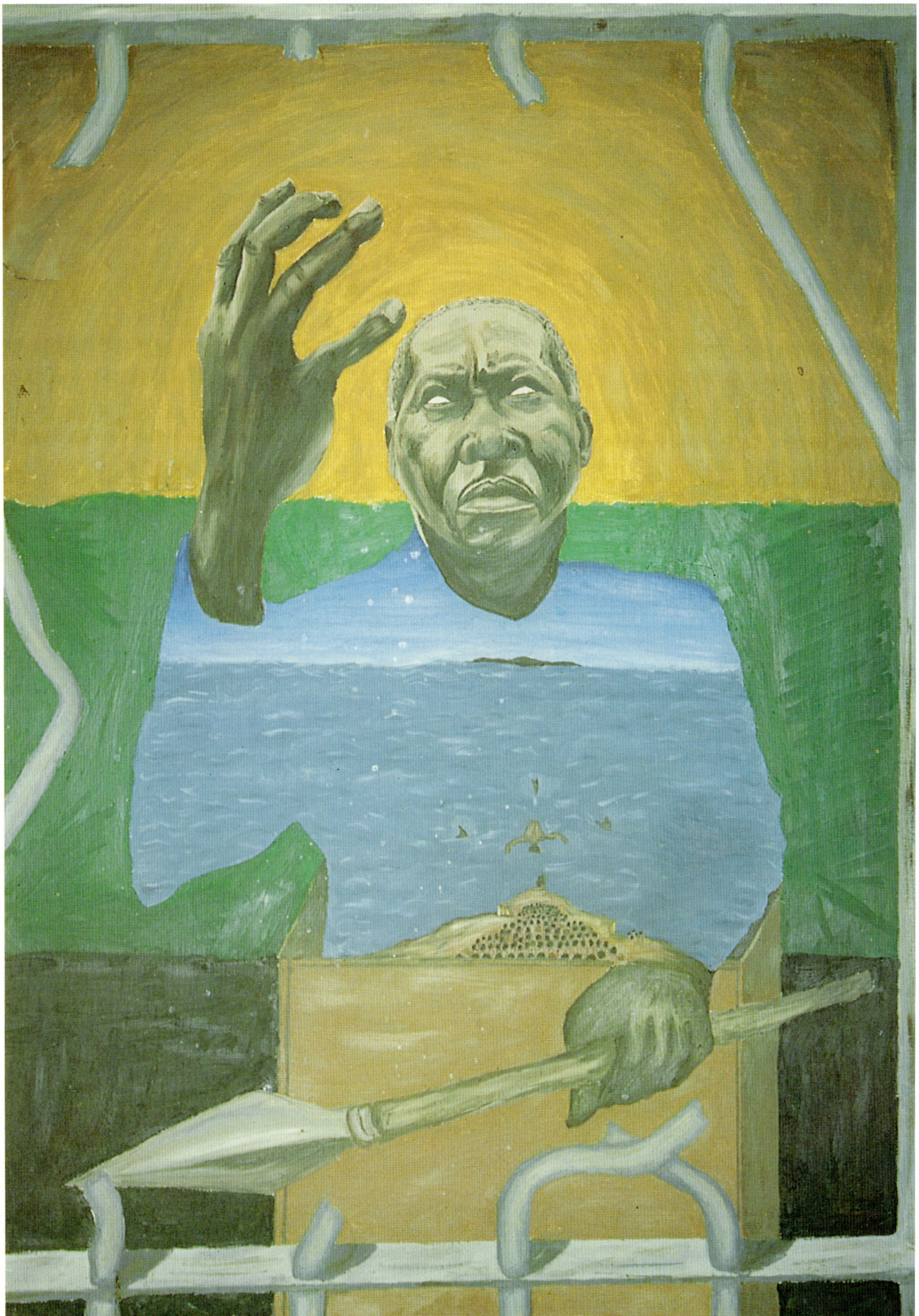

Mr close-friend-of-the-family pays a visit whilst everyone else is out
Charcoal on paper 109.2 x 150 cm
Sonia Boyce

BORN:
1962

NATIONALITY:
British

TYPE OF WORK:
drawings and paintings

Here is a very different sort of conflict. It involves a young girl. Have you ever had the feeling that something wrong is going to happen, and that the wrongdoer is someone you ought to be able to trust? What did you do?

Help is needed
Sonia Boyce, who drew this picture, thinks she knows what you would do. You look for help elsewhere, like the child who stares out of the picture at us with worried and fearful eyes. The idea for this picture came to Boyce when a well-known politician was said to have betrayed the trust of his voters. This made the artist think about powerful people and abuse, and made her remember incidents in her own life when she had felt threatened.

Boyce says that the picture has three people in it. These people are the child, the abuser and the viewer. One of the awful things about this sort of problem is that someone else often knows what is happening, but does nothing.

Simple and strong
Like Käthe Kollwitz, Boyce chose to make this picture in black and white. She felt that colour would confuse the idea. Instead, she relied upon the strength of contrasting light and dark. She has chosen a simple shape for the picture too — good on one side, bad on the other, the threatening arm linking the two. We cannot see the abuser's face. It is only the victim's emotions that we share. Behind the figures Boyce has painted a smooth and symmetrical pattern. Is it simply the comfortable wallpaper of a home? Is it there to make a deliberate contrast with the danger of the situation?

Caged in?
The picture is large, and is set inside a wide border. The border is an important part of the picture. The title trails menacingly around it, closing it in. Overlapping hands, some patterned, reach out from the sides. What do you think the artist meant these to say? Do they add to the threat or are they merely decoration?

© Sonia Boyce Arts Council Collection

The Schoolmaster

Oil on canvas 109 x 81 cm
Jan Steen

LIVED:
1625/6–79

NATIONALITY:
Dutch

TYPE OF WORK:
painting

Thyssen-Bornemisza Collection, Lugano, Switzerland

In Holland in the seventeenth century, life for many people was peaceful and prosperous. There was time for leisure, and money for comfortable homes and luxuries. Paintings were popular and in every town painters competed for trade. The people did not want grand, ornate works on their walls. They wanted simple paintings that reflected their surroundings. They liked local landscapes, realistic still-life paintings, portraits and scenes from their daily lives.

An observer of the people

Jan Steen painted everyday life. He made hundreds of pictures and was a popular artist. Not many artists became rich through their work, and Steen had to earn a living by keeping an inn.

Steen painted all sorts of people doing all sorts of things. He painted wealthy people in their elegant homes, working families sharing simple meals and jolly scenes of entertainers at inns. He painted people enjoying pastimes and games, and less happy scenes of squabbles and drunken brawls. It looks as though Steen enjoyed all the bustling life he observed. His pictures almost always show the funny side of life. He does not poke cruel fun but sees things lightheartedly. Perhaps it was his customers who wanted gaiety on the walls of their houses.

Conflict in the classroom

Steen's work has given us a detailed picture of life at the time. For instance, he painted several schoolroom scenes. This one shows the schoolmaster dealing with classroom conflict. Who drew lines all over the crumpled work on the floor? Perhaps the teacher, who looks as though he has come to the end of his patience, did it with the quill pen on his desk? Perhaps the weeping boy did it himself? The little girl at the desk with her reading book thinks the boy deserves the punishment anyway. The younger child beside her is not so sure. Perhaps he fears the same treatment. The smacking does not seem too unusual an event, because the children at the back of the room are taking no notice at all.

The National Gallery of Ireland

And When Did You Last See Your Father?

Oil on canvas 131 x 251 cm
William Frederick Yeames

LIVED:
1835–1918

NATIONALITY:
British

TYPE OF WORK:
historical paintings

Here is another child in trouble. This looks more serious than Jan Steen's trouble in the schoolroom. The little boy is not worried, but his sister is in tears and the women in the corner, perhaps his mother and older sister, look very troubled.

An imaginary event in an historic setting

The setting for this painting is the English Civil War (1642-1649) in which the Puritans defeated the Royalists, the supporters of the King, Charles I. Unlike Copley's painting, this is not a painting of a real event. It is an imaginary scene.

We can see from their clothing that the family in the picture are Royalists. The satin, velvet and lace, the bows and jewels, show which side they supported. The Puritans believed that such dress was sinful. They dressed plainly and Puritan women covered their hair.

The soldiers are searching for the owner of the house. The open chest on the left suggests that they have already searched it. Perhaps they have asked the lady where her husband is. Perhaps she has answered that he is away. The crafty soldier is not content with her answer. He checks by asking the children, 'And when did you last see your father?' What will the boy answer? Will he betray his father by telling the truth? Will he know that this time it might be right to lie?

A popular sentiment

William Frederick Yeames lived in the nineteenth century, 300 years after the Civil War had taken place. Historical paintings were very fashionable at the time, and the Civil War was the subject of many stories and plays. Queen Victoria had made the monarchy popular again, so the Royalists were seen as heroes. This sentimental painting shows the Puritan soldiers as dishonourable, trying to trick a child into betraying his father. The little boy with his straight back and honest look stands for bravery and innocence. Does his sister, a few years older than he is, understand what is going on or is she simply frightened by the soldiers in the house? In Victorian times, girls were often portrayed as weaker and more emotional than boys.

The Board of Trustees of the National Museums and Galleries on Merseyside (Walker Art Gallery)